Amy Todman

g(love)

SAD PRESS

Bristol 2019

978-1-912802-32-6

The cake shop is a landmark on my way to the path

There was snow on the mountains
in the distance and gathered at the side of the road.

(Outside I see pegs on wire

It was the first time and he wanted to feel it.
I tried to explain how snow feels in my hand. It is
surprising, hard to say.

moving past the bedroom window.

It is cold and then liquid in a warm hand, almost
burns
where crystals are packed and take longer to thaw.

I pin a map beside my bed
a pile of pink triangles in fragile construction, and I
hate maps).

The heat of my hand turns crystal to liquid.

I try to think about yellow circles but there is
nothing but triangles,
dusky with pomegranate juice, spread with my
pointing finger.

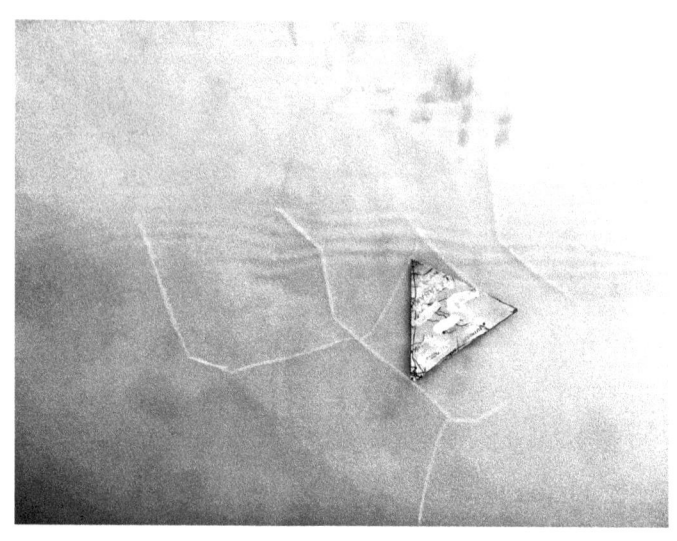

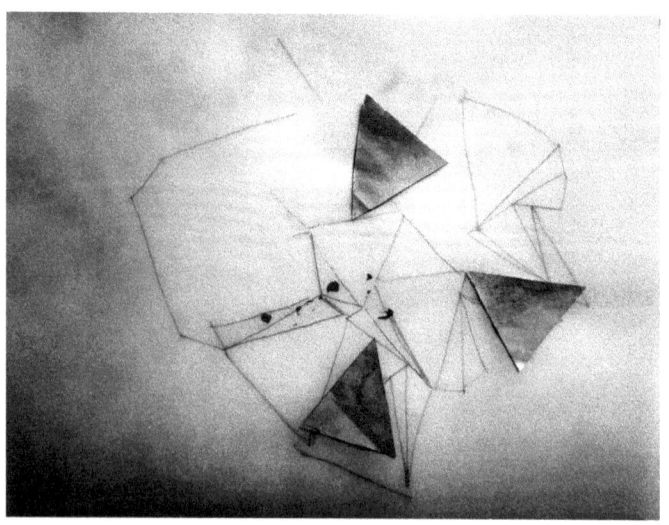

Stitched linen. Gorgeous, she might say.

Shoulder bag, hand bag, fingers bag.
Clutch.

Body bags. Linen skins.

Hard to bag before separation, requires a leap.

Stomach bag, thigh bag.

Parts with edges are more possible. Foot bag, for example.

I attach coloured ribbons to linen corners.
 - long streamers.

Some eel, she said. Cat toy for me. Pull me along. Jerk. Perfectly flat. Still.

Body bags. Linen skins. I pull you along, ribbons behind.
Empty.

Rustle. Pounce. She is captivated. Watches mouth part open.

Skin bag, bag of skin

fold crisp and iron through the night.
Incise.

Make geometry. Dry and scrape.
Hide. Thick as hide.

It rained, a sort of unsteady drip outside my window
all night. Her dog on instagram. Morning.

Yellow and yellow bowl. Butter   scotch.

Shred. Wed. Paper, bags and bags. Shed old skins.

Keratinocytes
dermis
subcutis.

Fold crisp and iron linen through the night.
Absorbing. Cool and freshly

linen trousers. Drawstring.

Long staple.

I made a hand bag today.

Linen square
sewn up three sides
and open at the top
with a frayed edge.

I put my closed fist inside.

A stone picked up from the causeway at low tide.

Scored face. White in grooves.

On the floor near the bed, I catch a white flicker
and look again as I walk to the window.
Sandra is in the chair watching the light.

That stone how can it fit the linen squares –
light and unfettered.

The heavy stone. Wind does nothing. Why pick it
up?

Listen. Its white scored face.

Place stone on linen, wrap without covering. Wrap
to reveal.

It may come to nothing.

A lesser black back gull's nest
Patrick tells me
I have no idea.

I nearly stand on it balancing on the pointed rocks.
Behind me a linen shroud for rock.

buffets in the wind
fabric flattens hard
then flaps. Madly.

We are watching the FA cup
Patrick is.

I write down about the black back gull.

I dreamed the folds. It shrouds.
Should shroud.

Dream fold. Wake.

Iron that linen iron. Linen.
Jesus. Linen.

Download 1754 images from my iphone. It takes forever
and so I keep ironing.

Iron out those creases. Sea. Crease.

Iron. Flat. Add water. Steam.

Turn. Iron.

The ironing board is made for shirt sleeves but here I am ironing a linen shroud.

Fold. Iron. Fold. Iron. Add water. Fold. Iron. Fold. Iron.

Press. In my dream it was linen on white I think.

The folded cloth was with me when I woke up.

A visitation, a prayer in silver.

I am here before the folded linen, which we have called shroud. I have already written it into a poem – folded shroud – and it is just

I am somewhat in love with the linen
folded this way.

From this angle, kneeling on the rug resting on my elbows to write, the frayed edges are so. So visible.

On that long side (I am almost looking at the nearest corner so I can see both long and short sides clearly and I am just above them) the frayed edges and loose threads (curling flatly where they have been carefully ironed) obscure the layers so it is hard to count them, if you want to.

But the short side shows blunt folds, dark undersides (I passed the iron back and forth over these gradually smoothing edges this morning, early, after the dream woke me. The linen square had been crumpled in a plastic bag along with other cloth and some sand in the bottom) and I can see four folds and maybe four frayed edges.

The fabric is so. So flat. So. So silver.

Spread that square out on the sand. Spread and ruffle. Wind. Everything open not bare but. So. Silver.

I cried.

And now home fold. Press. Fold. Press. Fold.

Press. A shroud cares for ritual.

Are people cruel.

Yes, of course, they can be. I can be.

Defenceless love.

Love, a defenceless position.

I just get happy. Is this happy?

WORDGLOVE
GLOVEWORD

My heart is breaking, I think, in the kitchen just wiping down the surfaces.

Or my chest is breaking.

(Love. Or panic)

This GLOVEWORD WORDGLOVE really needs a life. This linen. This creased and flat. This cursive and unpicked with a blade.

The word was glove.
The glove did not fit the hand.

The glove is light, unburdened, though the word is heavy.

OH G (LOVE)

I move away. The word is heavy but the glove is light. It is not a glove. I unpicked it but even before it was a useless glove. Never meant to be a glove. What is a useless glove? What is a purposefully useless glove.

Love, but so light.

So heavy, the word.

I look but I cannot see what object it might have been or want to be

It has landscape qualities
perhaps a painting - a hill, or a contour

Then I can see it on the wall of some stately home
surrounded by a large frame.

But from here it is a flat piece of cloth. Muslin and
linen pieces laid on by me
and I must name. Yes like we all

- all I can do then with this flat thing
is to write that name backwards in thread with
great cursive care
turn it so the back is at the front

- eman

and then on the surface

 - no

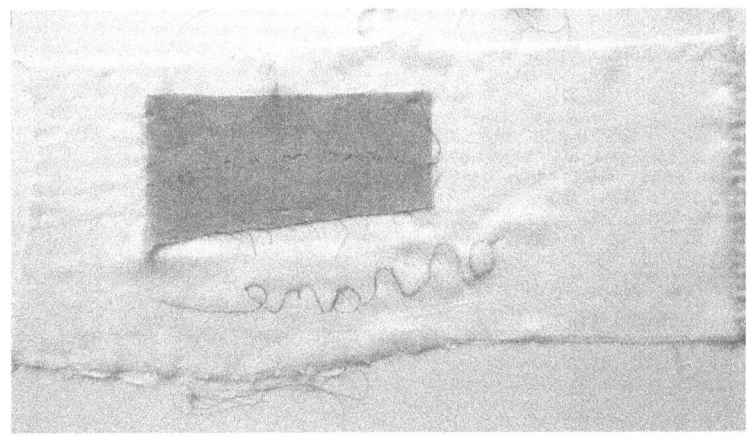

It turns
~~the garden~~ crossed out
cleared   (branch

light

    and becoming structure)

July begins:

Rose, peony, lavender
        crabapple.

      Hayfever.

Arms (scratch
red knuckle

meat under skin
scratch.   pull and

Split rib-cage thick white bone).

There is a poem for everything and we want a badge
to say We Work
From First Principles.

I feel

burn what you
(drawn in

what   love
what

what hot heat

~~Ash~~ I crossed this out.

What cool white powder.
Coil).

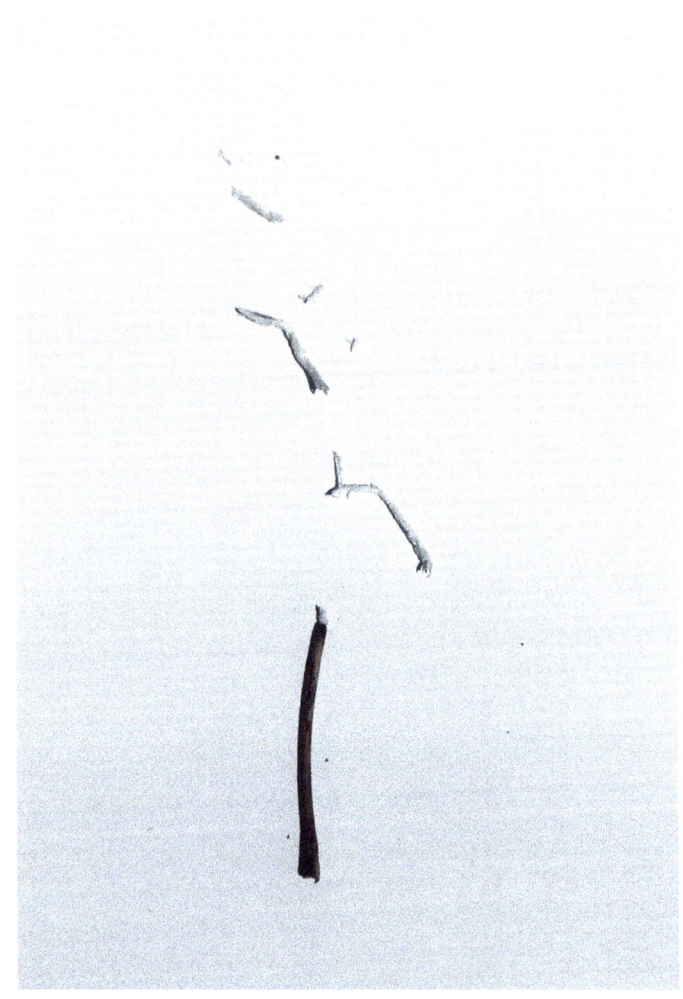

I read Sharon Olds poems about her mother
and I am surprised she goes so far.
It's not awkward for me

but if it was.

    What is too far (for this poem.

Ash.

What is
  this ash

what did I burn

some part of mine
and what did I not burn).

I burned a sculpture, a cotton sculpture. It was
white. I had sewed the word soft in large letters in
dark blue cotton thread across the centre. And the
word hard in red cotton thread over the top. The
two words overlapped but my five year old niece
could still make them out.

I burnt my soft in a   pɹɐɥ   small fire on the
back step in the sun
into a saucepan a third full of water

The ash did not fall neatly. I picked it out of the
water in a clump and hung it on the line.
brought into the living room and flattened onto
paper, smoothing with my hands.

Ashy hands. Soft
hard nuggets. Cremain like

There.

It's just my dead body
burned in the sun, flattened under paper

At 1.31 I wake up and consider going to sit on the back step in the dark. The word untethered. In three days Armenia.

I have been alone this week, holding my head. It's where I want to be. It's not where I want to be.

After such a peace.

I have put away everything. A suitcase and a large bag. I don't know why I am going except not knowing why I am going.

There is no great consolidation. And yet there are

I like the random word generator. It speaks the way I would speak. Woold.

On the wall (and it is orange dark) the cupboard slants. That's not amazing. That is amazing.

I am so angry. I am not so angry.

The instructions. I heard both sides when I sat. Both confirmed my stupidity, I can't remember why.

I banged them together and there was silence. Absence. If I am not stupid

There was a roll of thick silver tape left on the table

(I've been packing for days and still there are piles (small, awkward piles of objects that don't fit their spaces) on surfaces and floors and the table.

I tore off a small piece of tape (tore surprisingly well, after I gnawed a little) and used it to shape an unfolded cardboard box (maybe it was a lemon and ginger tea bag box, or herbal nytol) into a sort of ball. I only needed small pieces of tape here and there. I was careful.

Later the ball was on the coffee table, beside a cardboard and tape pole, sort of like a scaled down, grey maypole. From the other side of the room maybe they look like nothing, or they just look like they shouldn't be there (shouldn't)

Overpowering, however they look. Not meant to be there is a large frame.

Small stick and ball, made of what was left after packing.

Share, expose nothing much but the part that
would be public
but public only if framed by practice.

In this more unbounded way it *is* exposing (or it
would always be exposing but I forget)

Framing is containing. That's obvious. But this is
framed too, pictures float. Past.

Unframed, they are unseen and so *not* exposed.

But then in the framing of the photograph they are
seen differently
I want to expose *that* seeing. That differently.

I want framing to make visible but not project what

I do not like projection. Falsehood. Something not
yet there
Project an image. Project yourself. Be a project
manager. Be someone's project.

An alternative, or perhaps addition, to projection:
Project yourself partially. At least that gives wiggle
room. Project a partial.

sad, grey maypole and a lone dancer. It is a tap and
ball at the corner of the white screen.

here is something

(locating is hard   It is like

> The map locates me on the globe. I have looked into that.

I locate myself.

First the Colombian, the Colombian in
Prague
me on the streets and you, not the
Colombian, on chat.
Waving line. More than one of you, waving.

Later I gave the Colombian a name.
It was a jerk.
Gap, then press the bent arrow.

The Colombian stopped me explaining too much. The Colombian kept our distance.

I called him by his name when we spoke on chat. Not to him, but to you. I don't know what he called me.

I'm from Scotland but I don't know if he called me that.

language stubs. Like stubbing my toe on the path. Stubbing my words).

There is no great consolidation (only

great bites. Bit.
Spit into an exact location.

Imagine a bite (apple)
hard and a little juicy.
Take the lump from your mouth and push it on the
fruit.

Like fingernails now cool and hard, dislocated
spikes in my fingers.
Not warm pliable stubs attached to skin.

somewhere) pulls them in
spread across my desktop and table.